Papeterie Bleu

SHARE the LOVE
an ADULT COLOURING BOOK

Want free goodies?
Email us at freebies@pbleu.com

@papeteriebleu

Papeterie Bleu

Shop our other books at
www.pbleu.com

Wholesale distribution through Ingram Content Group
www.ingramcontent.com/publishers/distribution/wholesale

For questions and customer service, email us at
support@pbleu.com

FREE PDF DOWNLOAD OF THIS BOOK

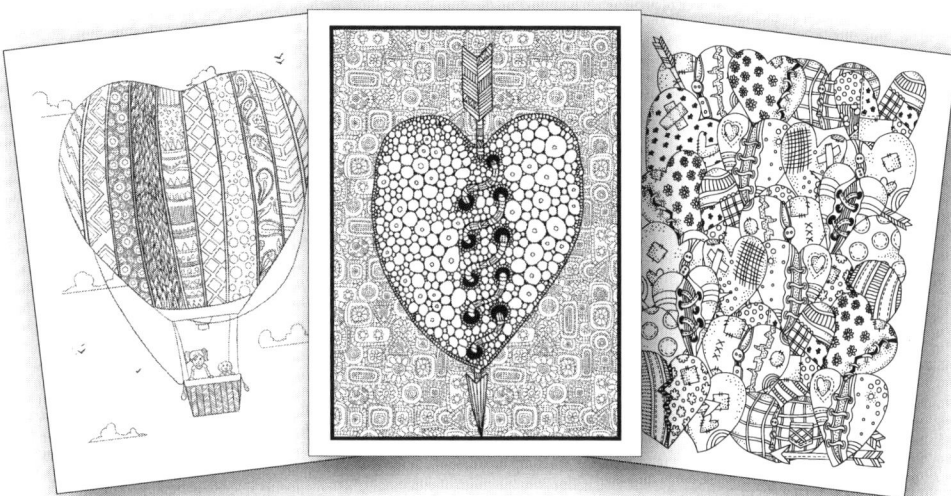

www.pbleu.com/stleng

YOUR DOWNLOAD CODE: STL7695

@papeteriebleu

Papeterie Bleu

LOVE PLANTED A ROSE,
AND THE WORLD TURNED SWEET.

- KATHARINE LEE BATES -

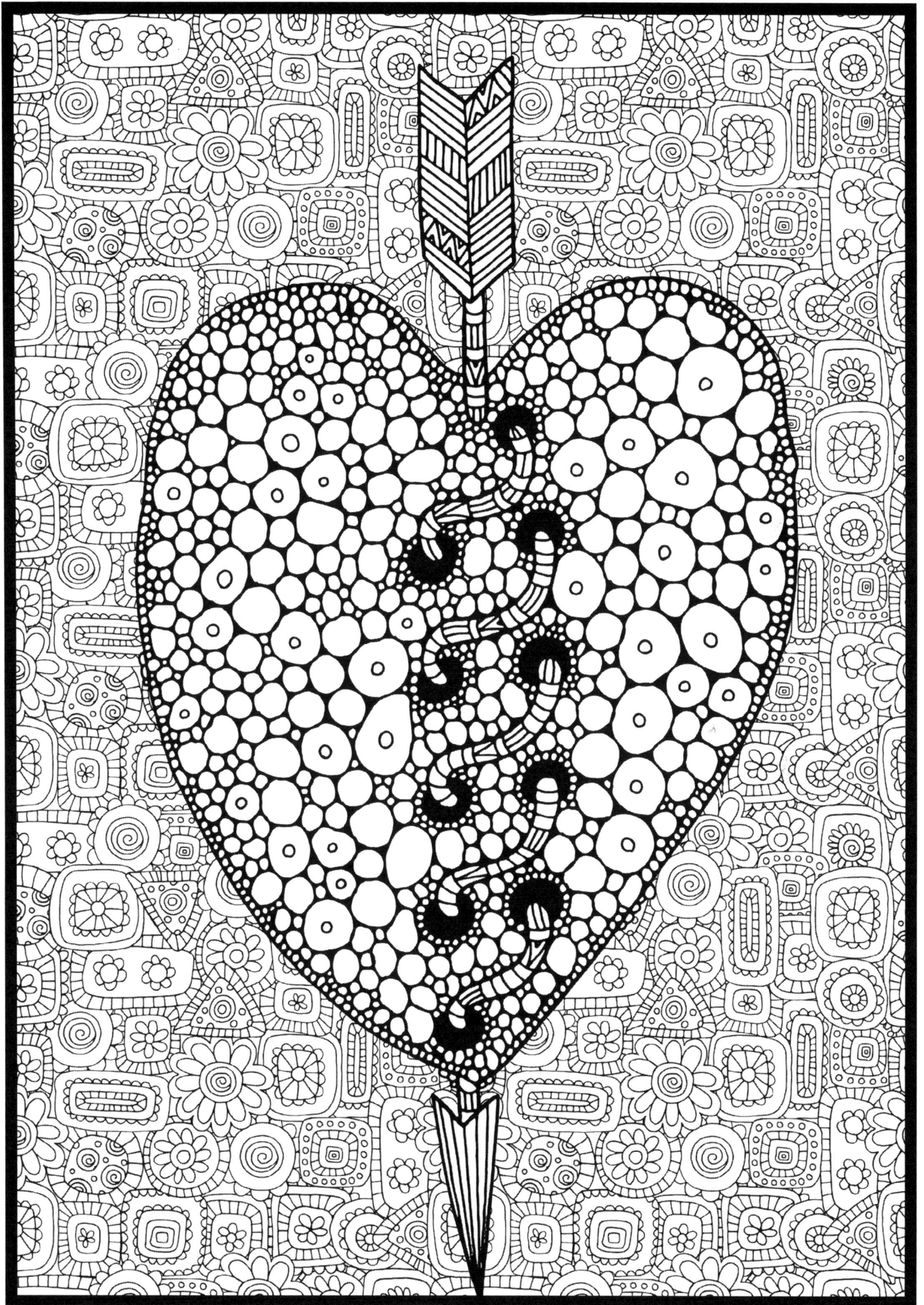

LOVE IS LIKE THE WIND,
YOU CAN'T SEE IT,
BUT YOU CAN FEEL IT.

- NICHOLAS SPARKS -

LOVE ALL, TRUST FEW,
DO WRONG TO NONE.

- WILLIAM SHAKESPEARE -

IN DREAMS AND IN LOVE,
THERE ARE
NO IMPOSSIBILITIES.

- JANOS ARANY -

KEEP LOVE IN YOUR HEART.
A LIFE WITHOUT IT IS LIKE
A SUNLESS GARDEN WHEN
THE FLOWERS ARE DEAD.

- OSCAR WILDE -

IT IS BETTER TO LOVE WISELY,
NO DOUBT: BUT TO LOVE
FOOLISHLY IS BETTER THAN NOT
TO BE ABLE
TO LOVE AT ALL.

- WILLIAM MAKEPEACE THACKERAY -

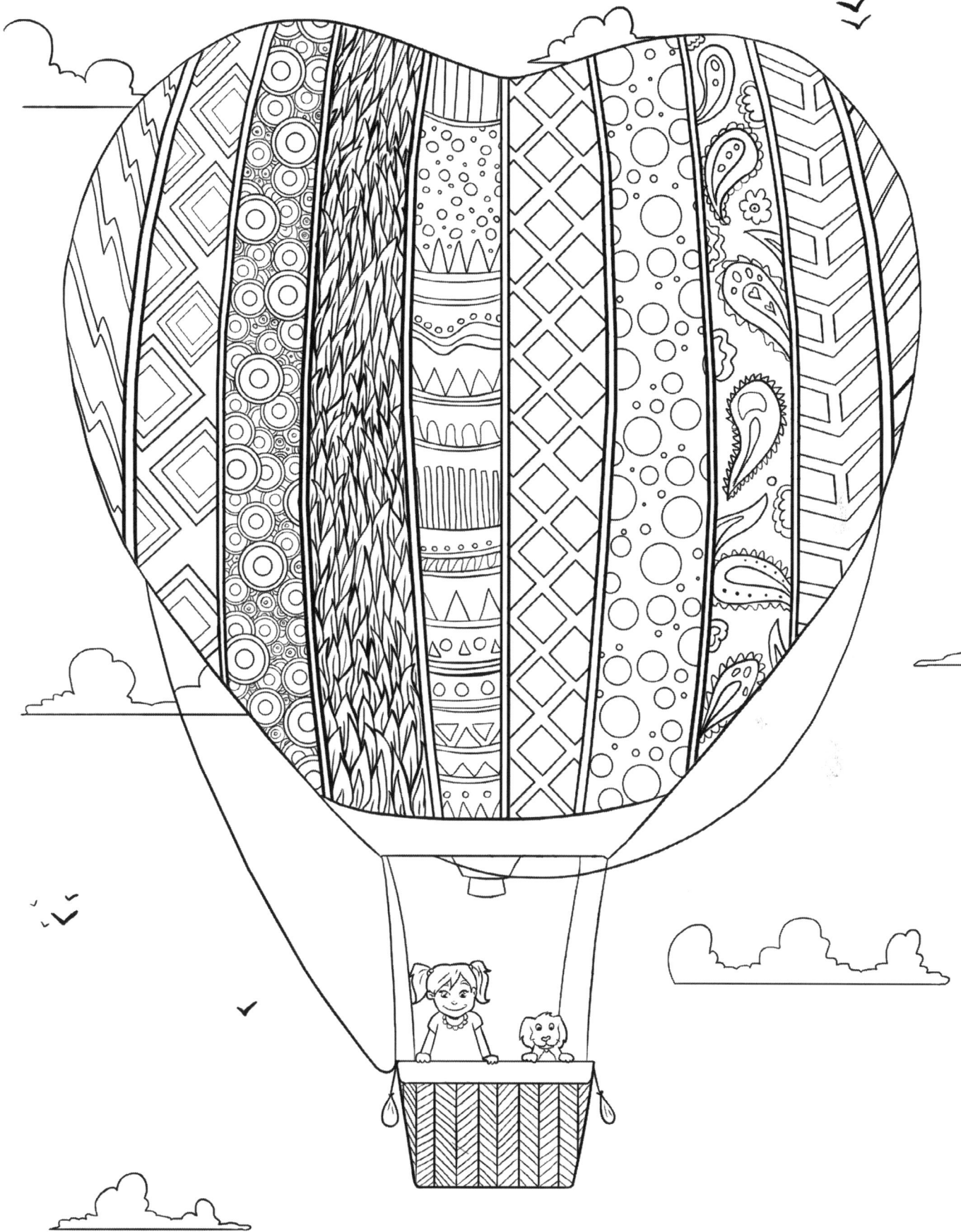

LOVE IS THAT CONDITION
IN WHICH THE HAPPINESS
OF ANOTHER PERSON
IS ESSENTIAL TO YOUR OWN.

- ROBERT HEINLEIN -

WE'RE ALL A LITTLE WEIRD,
AND LIFE'S A LITTLE WEIRD.
AND WHEN WE FIND SOMEONE
WHOSE WEIRDNESS IS COMPATIBLE
WITH OURS, WE JOIN UP WITH
THEM AND FALL IN MUTUAL
WEIRDNESS AND CALL IT LOVE.

- DR. SEUSS -

I CAN LIVE WITHOUT MONEY,
BUT I CANNOT LIVE WITHOUT
LOVE.

- JUDY GARLAND -

LOVE DOESN'T MAKE
THE WORLD GO ROUND.
LOVE IS WHAT MAKES
THE RIDE WORTHWHILE.

- FRANKLIN P. JONES -

ALL YOU NEED IS LOVE.
BUT A LITTLE CHOCOLATE
NOW AND THEN DOESN'T HURT.

- CHARLES SCHULZ -

TO LOVE
AND BE LOVED
IS TO FEEL THE SUN
FROM BOTH SIDES.

- DAVID VISCOTT -

A FLOWER CANNOT BLOSSOM
WITHOUT SUNSHINE, AND MAN
CANNOT LIVE WITHOUT LOVE.

- MAX MULLER -

LOVE IS OUR TRUE DESTINY.
WE DO NOT FIND THE MEANING
OF LIFE BY OURSELVES ALONE —
WE FIND IT WITH ANOTHER.

- THOMAS MERTON -

LIFE IS A FLOWER
OF WHICH LOVE IS
THE HONEY.

- VICTOR HUGO -

DARKNESS CANNOT DRIVE OUT
DARKNESS: ONLY LIGHT CAN DO
THAT. HATE CANNOT DRIVE OUT
HATE: ONLY LOVE CAN DO THAT.

- MARTIN LUTHER KING, JR. -

LOVE IS A GAME
THAT TWO CAN PLAY
AND BOTH WIN.

- EVA GABOR -

THE GREATEST HEALING THERAPY
IS FRIENDSHIP AND LOVE.

- HUBERT H. HUMPHREY -

LOVE IS A FRIENDSHIP
SET TO MUSIC.

- E. JOSEPH COSSMAN -

THERE IS ONLY ONE
HAPPINESS IS THIS LIFE,
TO LOVE AND BE LOVED.

- GEORGE SAND -

LOVE IS OF ALL PASSIONS
THE STRONGEST, FOR IT ATTACKS
SIMULTANEOUSLY THE HEAD,
THE HEART, AND THE SENSES.

- LAO TZU -

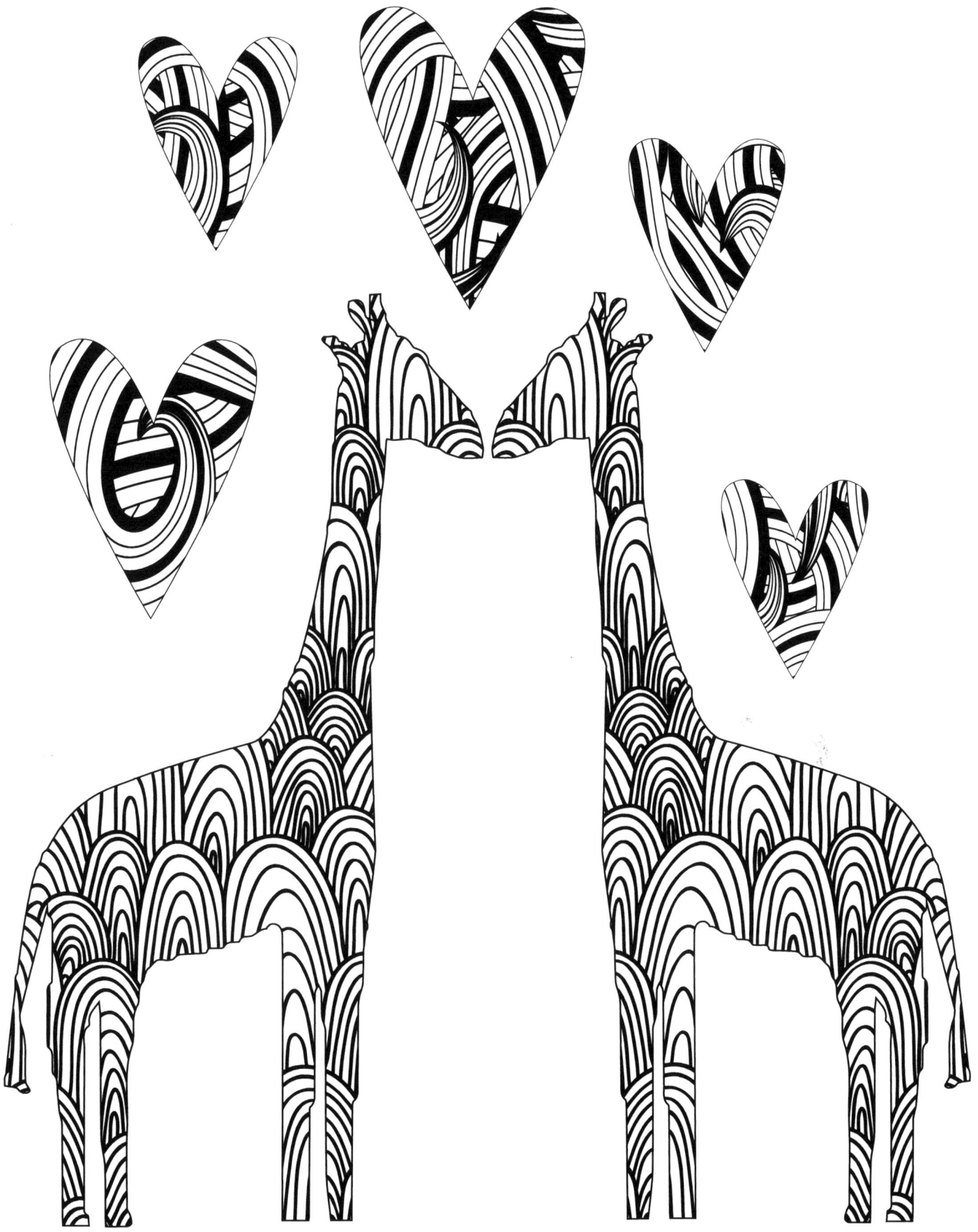

THE MORE I THINK ABOUT IT,
THE MORE I REALIZE THERE
IS NOTHING MORE ARTISTIC
THAN TO LOVE OTHERS.

- VINCENT VAN GOGH -

LOVE IS WHEN THE OTHER
PERSON'S HAPPINESS IS MORE
IMPORTANT THAN YOUR OWN.

- H. JACKSON BROWN, JR. -

With love

FRIENDS SHOW THEIR LOVE
IN TIMES OF TROUBLE,
NOT IN HAPPINESS.

- EURIPIDES -

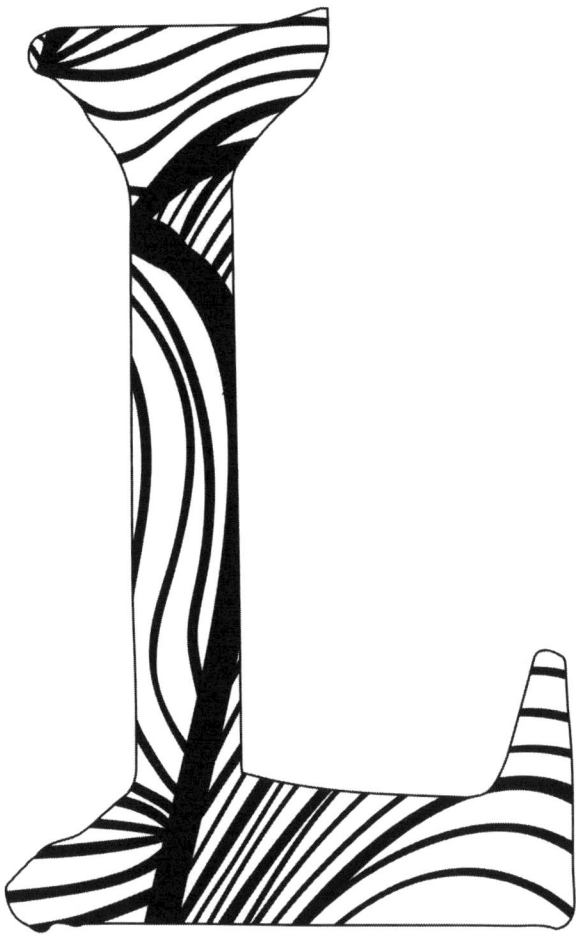

LOVE IS THE ONLY FORCE
CAPABLE OF TRANSFORMING
AN ENEMY INTO A FRIEND.

- MARTIN LUTHER KING, JR -

BEING DEEPLY LOVED
BY SOMEONE GIVES YOU STRENGTH,
WHILE LOVING SOMEONE DEEPLY
GIVES YOU COURAGE.

- LAO TZU -

THE MOST IMPORTANT THING
IN THE WORLD IS FAMILY AND
LOVE.

- JOHN WOODEN -

I HAVE FOUND THAT IF YOU LOVE
LIFE, LIFE WILL LOVE YOU BACK.

- ARTHUR RUBINSTEIN -

LOVE IS BUT THE DISCOVERY
OF OURSELVES IN OTHERS,
AND THE DELIGHT IN THE
RECOGNITION.

- ALEXANDER SMITH -

LOVE KEEPS THE COLD OUT BETTER
THAN A CLOAK

- HENRY WADSWORTH LONGFELLOW -

LOVE IS THE GREATEST
REFRESHMENT IN LIFE.

- PABLO PICASSO -

LOVE LOVES TO LOVE LOVE.

- JAMES JOYCE -

FREE PDF DOWNLOAD OF THIS BOOK

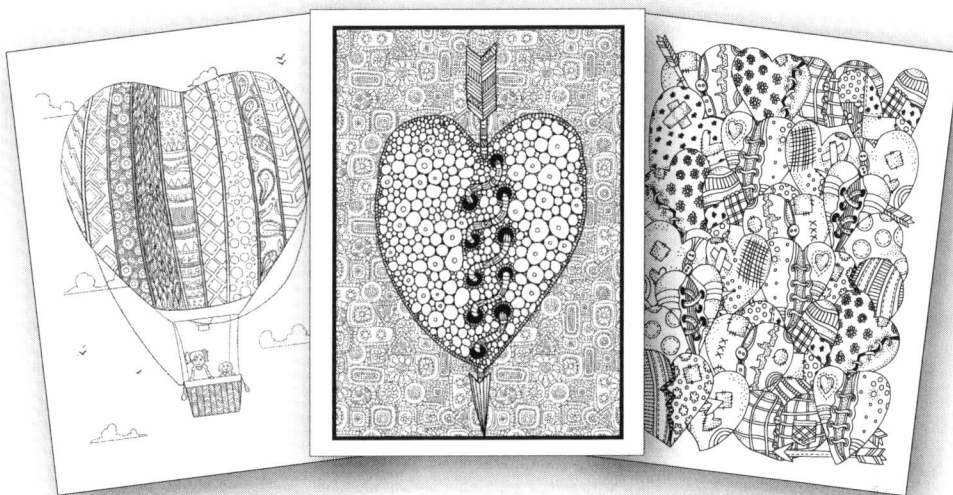

www.pbleu.com/stleng

YOUR DOWNLOAD CODE: STL7695

@papeteriebleu

Papeterie Bleu

Printed in Great Britain
by Amazon